I0494603

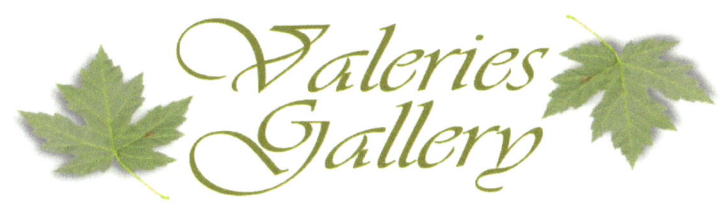

PICTURES AND POEMS

By

Valerie Taplin

Published By Mind Your Head UK
United Kingdom
www.MindYourHeadUK.com

First Edition

ISBN   978-0-9556935-1-9

www.Valeries-Gallery.co.uk

Introduction

Valerie has been a keen photographer for many years and living below the South Downs in England she uses every opportunity she can to capture the beautiful countryside on camera, many photos of which can be viewed on her website www.valeries-gallery.co.uk.

These photographs together with her love of writing poetry have enabled her to blend this lovely combination and create this book for all to enjoy.

I walked along the bluebell glade
In colours soft and blue
The flowers bowed their tender heads
To greet the morning dew

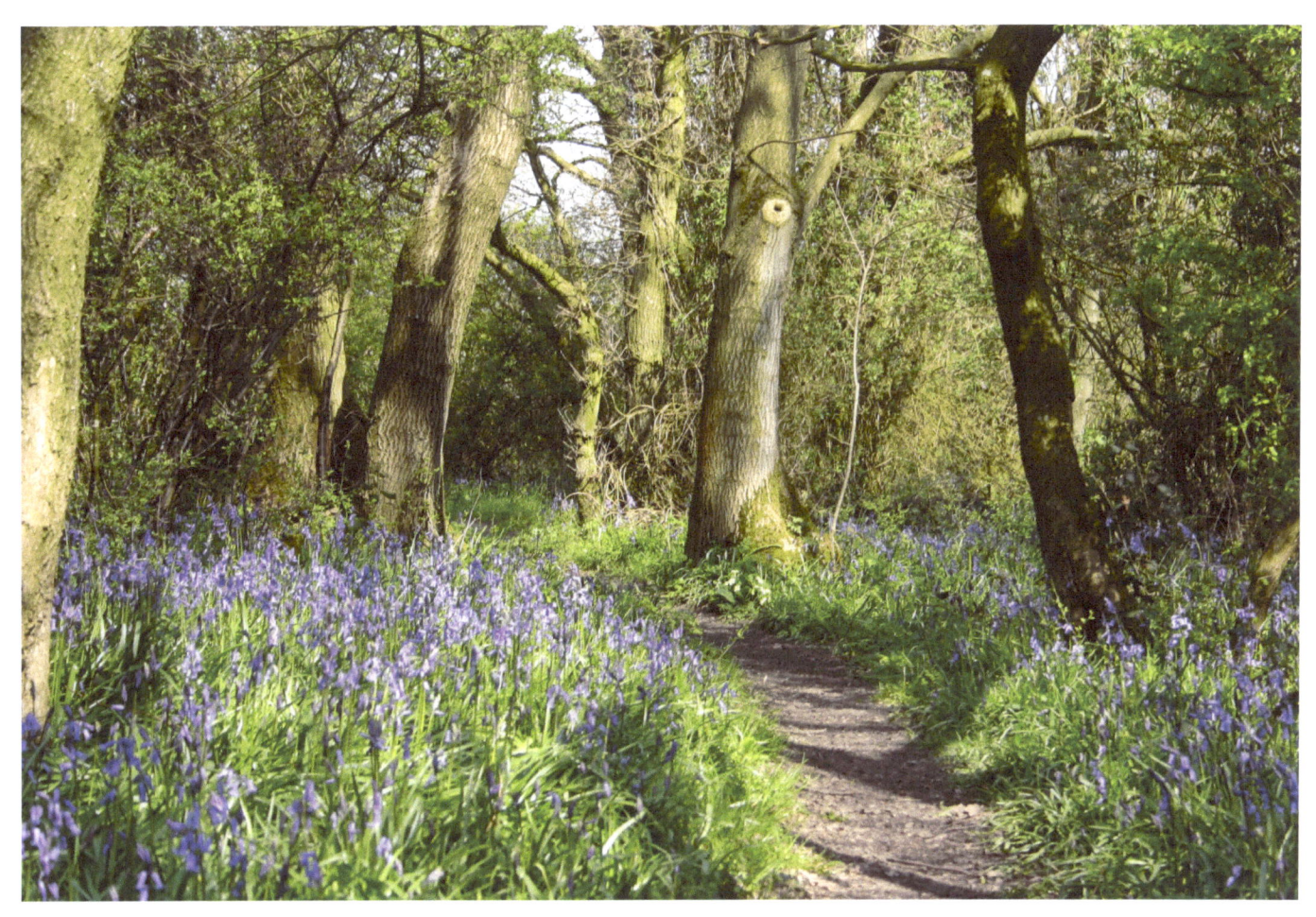

Bluebell Glade

I stood beneath the shady tree
And who should come to greet me
My friends who seem to know my face
And join me at the meeting place

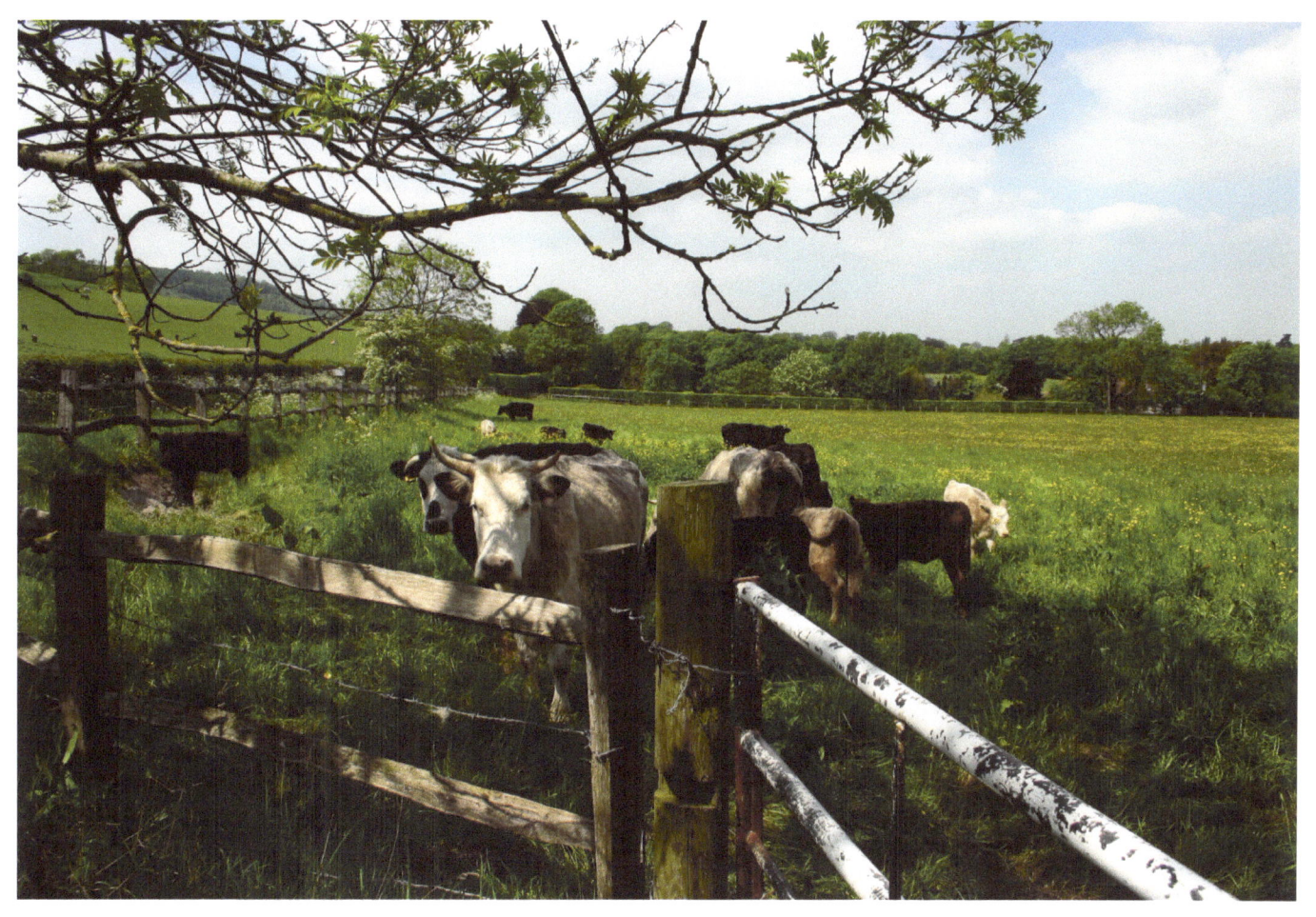

The Meeting Place

Poppies swaying to and fro
In the wind their petals flow
Like tissue paper in the breeze
The red heads beckon to the bees.

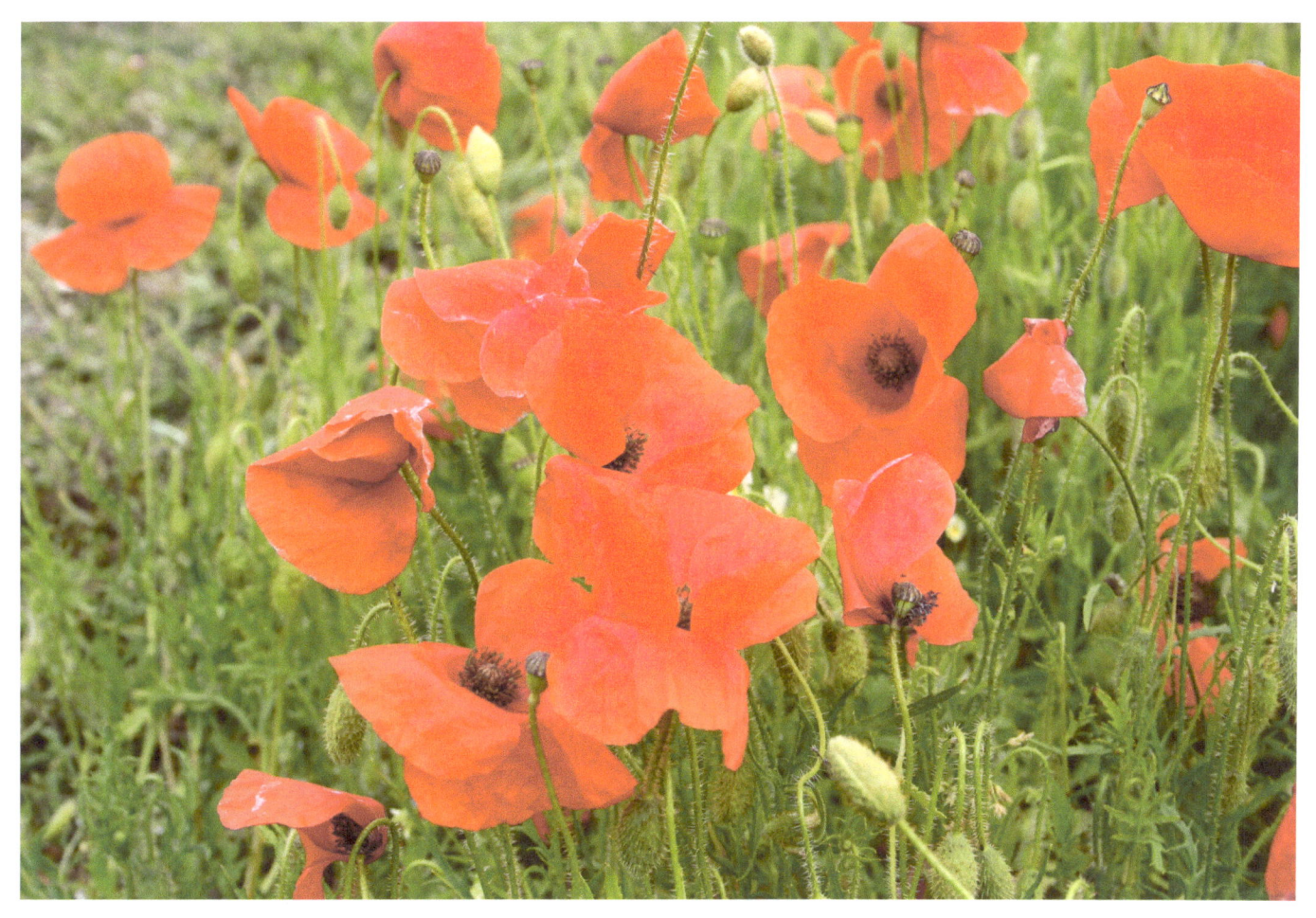

Red Heads

Summers come and summers go
Their warmth will still remain
The farmers sing a loud hay-ho
To celebrate the grain

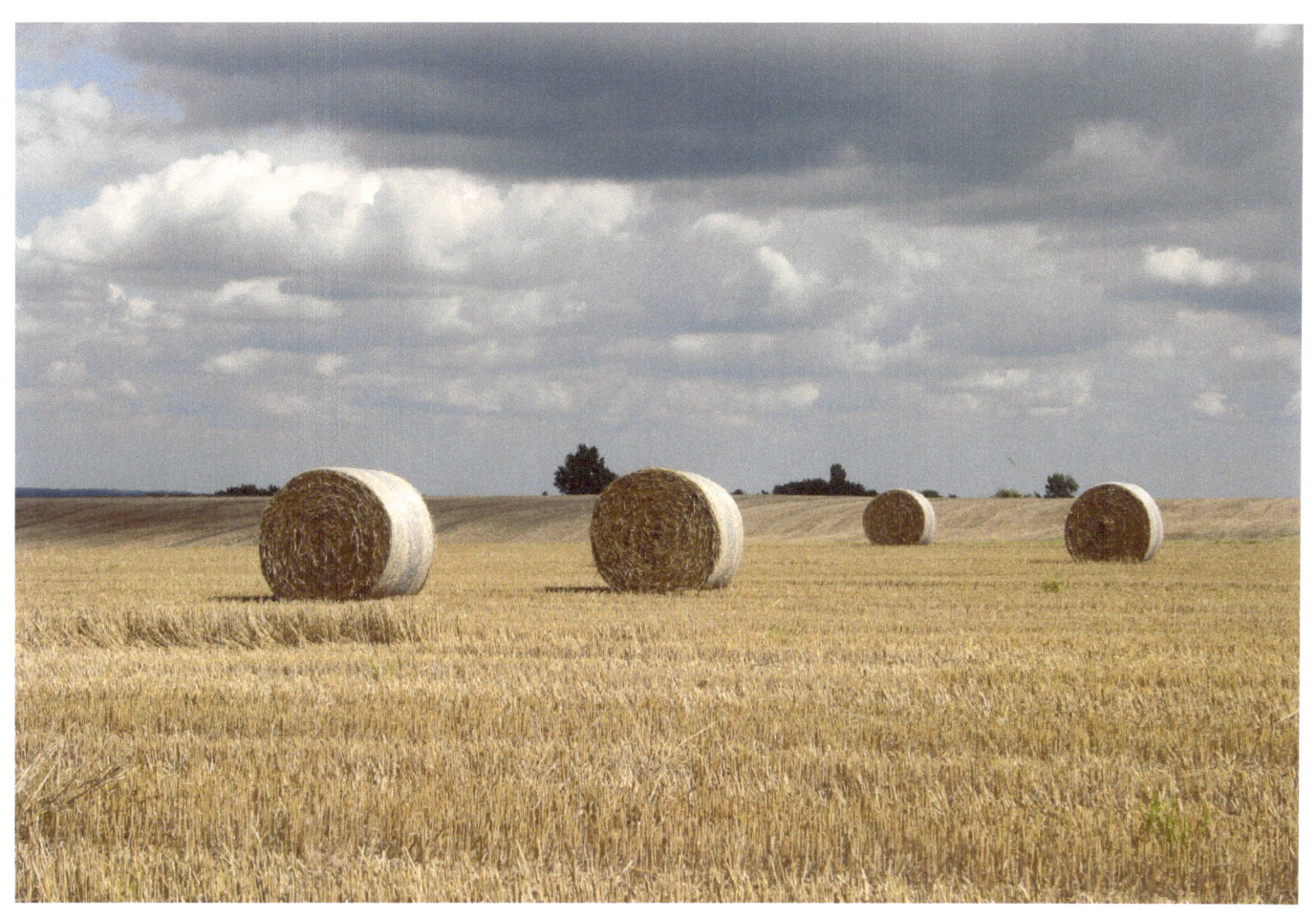

Hay ho

Get your sledges, get your trays
And join us on the Downs
The snow has come and we'll have fun
On the big toboggan run

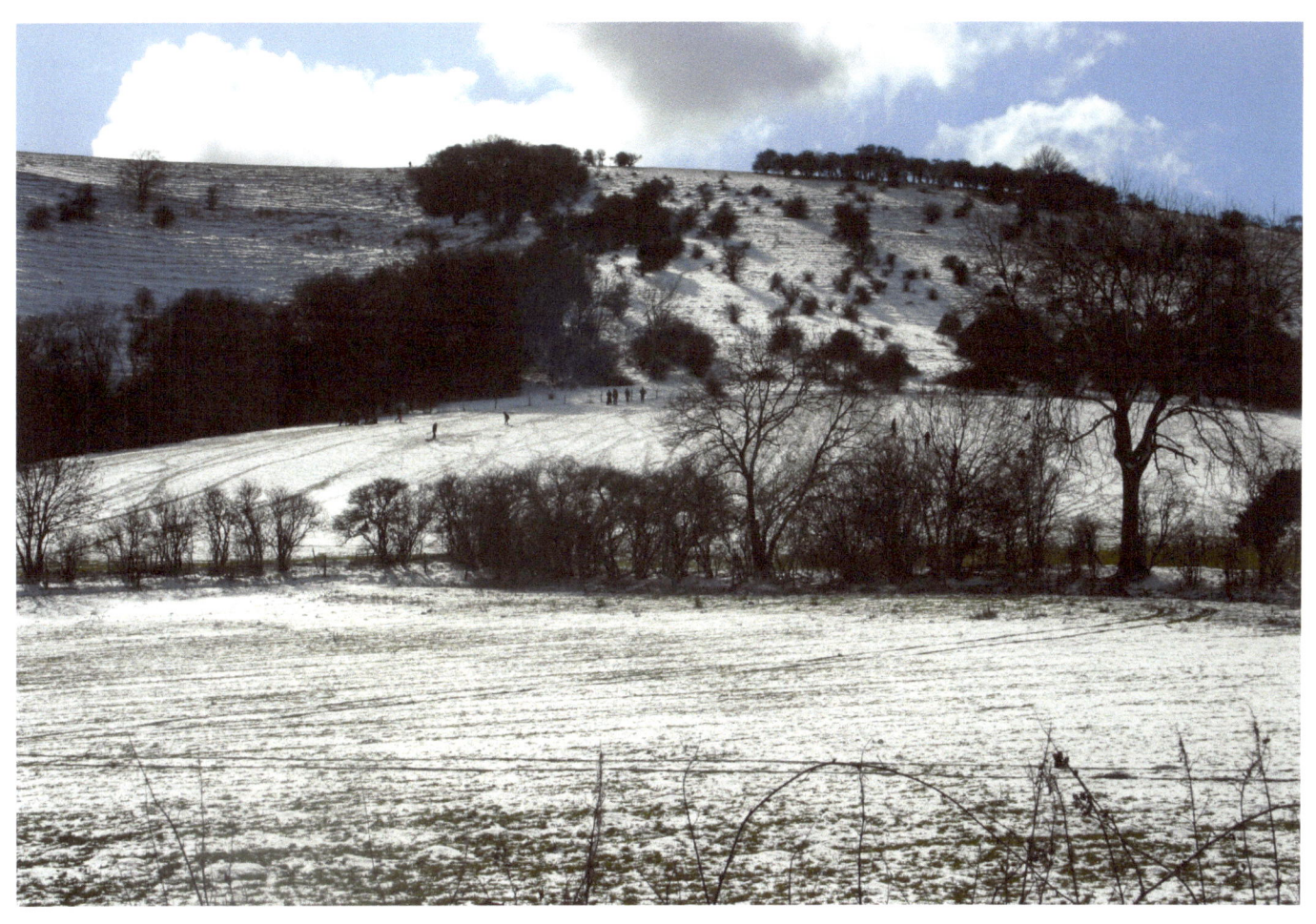

Toboggan Run

Clucking here and clucking there
The chicken chums are meeting
The cockerel crowing loud and clear
To give his morning greeting

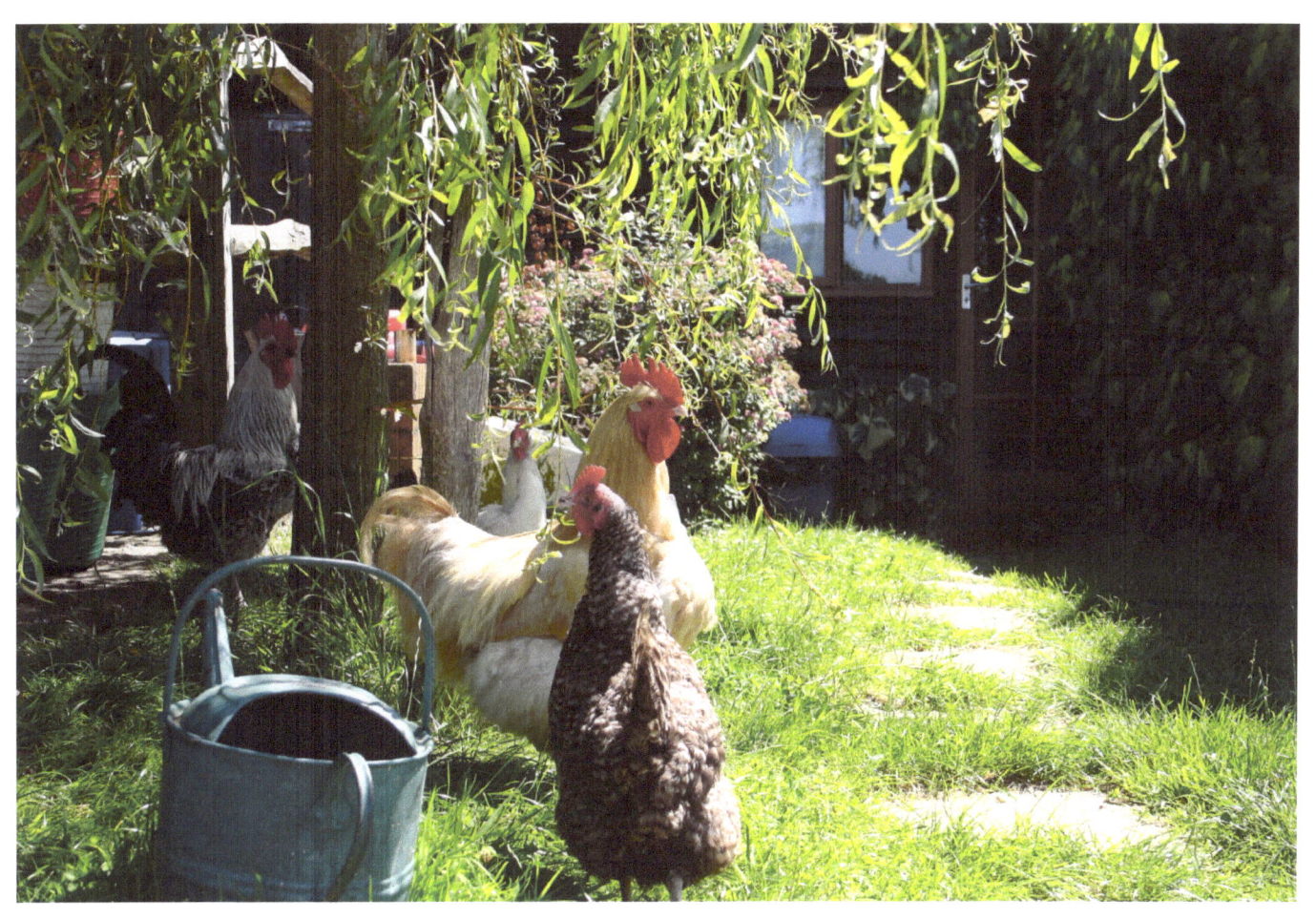

Chicken Chums

The secret garden draws me close
And makes me want to see
What lies around the corner
And beyond the old oak tree

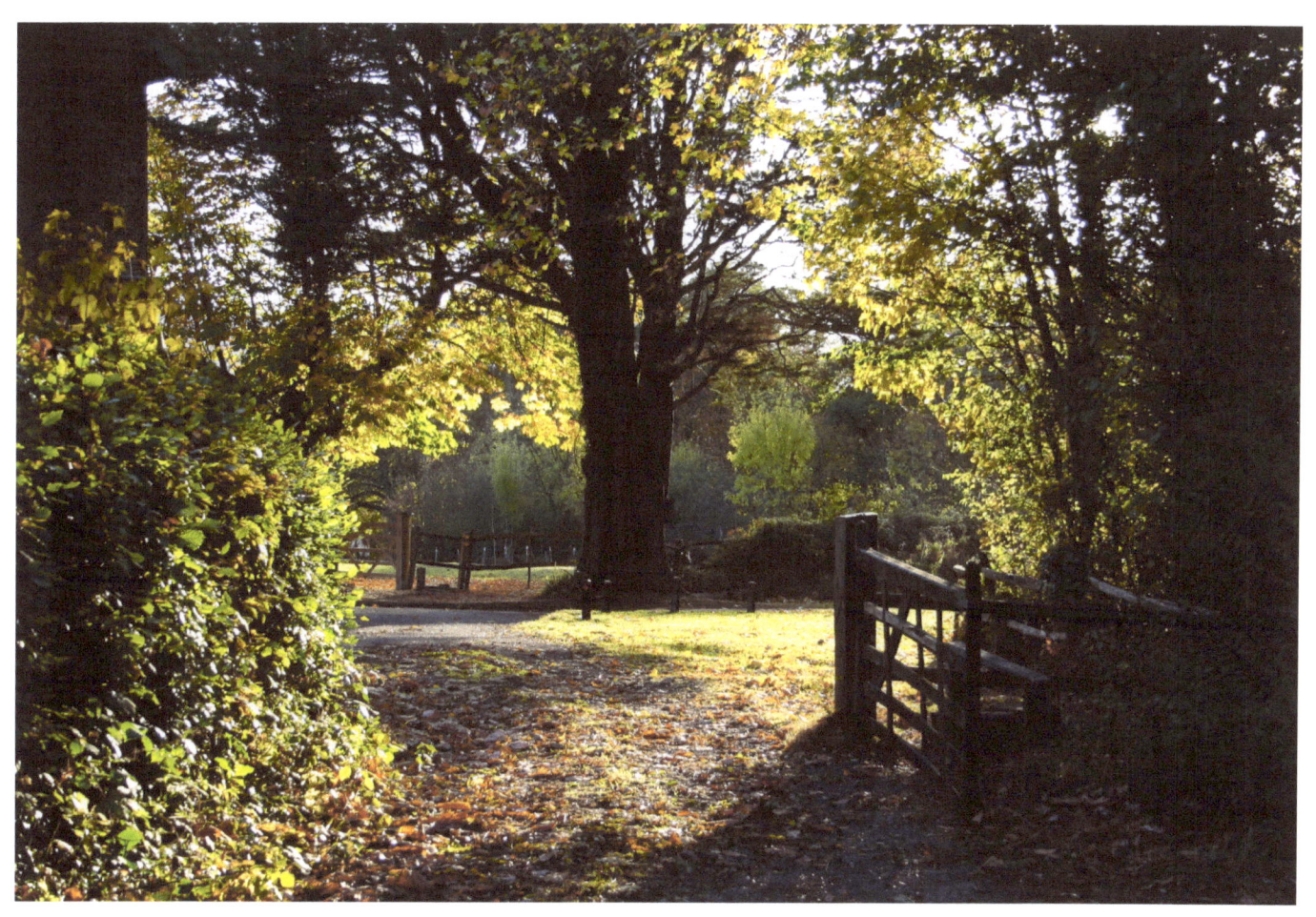

The Secret Garden

The primroses, the bluebells too
Blending yellow with the blue
On the spring bank wild and free
Putting on a show for me

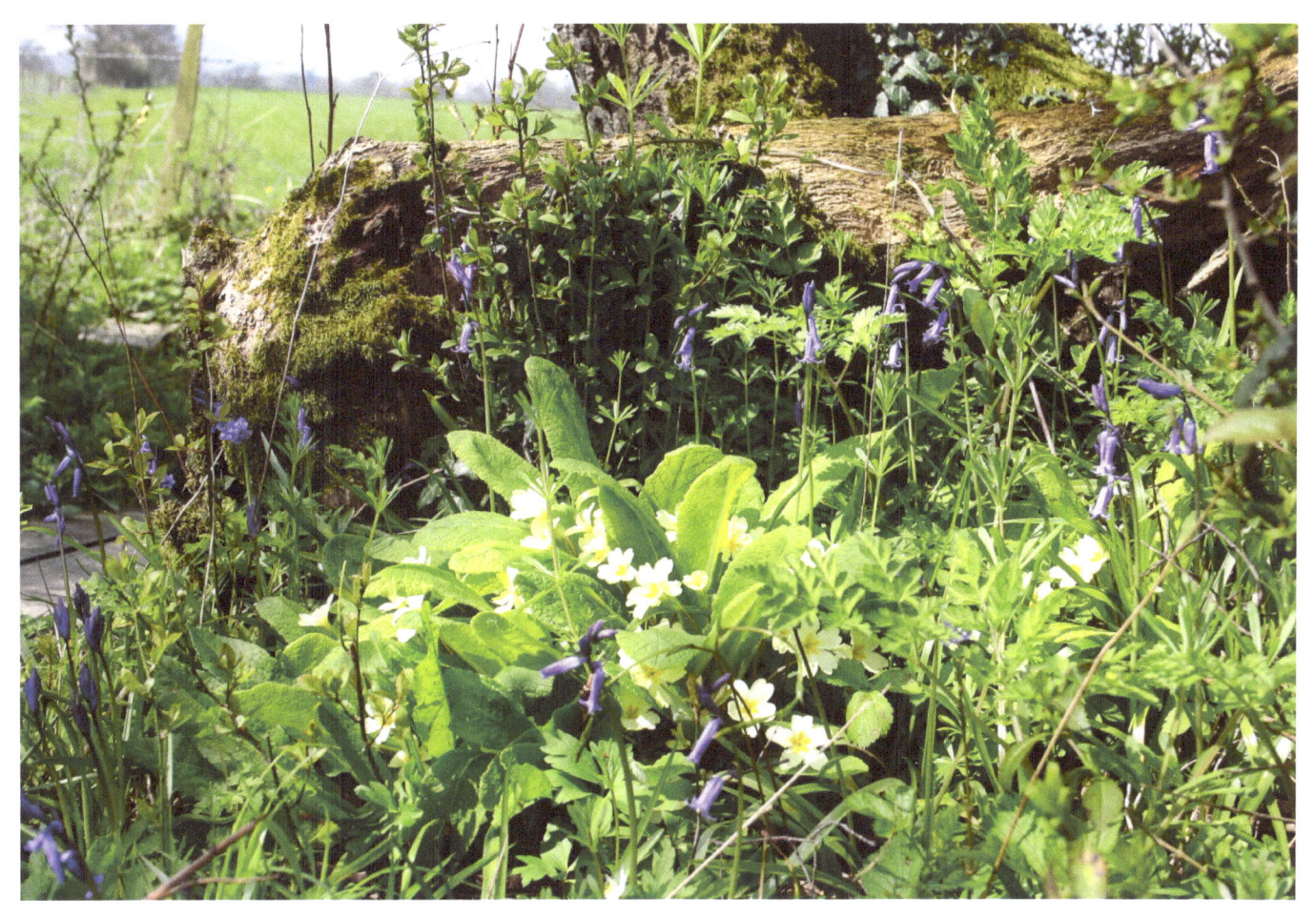

Spring Bank

What a view this lady has
Who looks down from the hill
To see the seasons come and go
Her name of course, Jill Mill

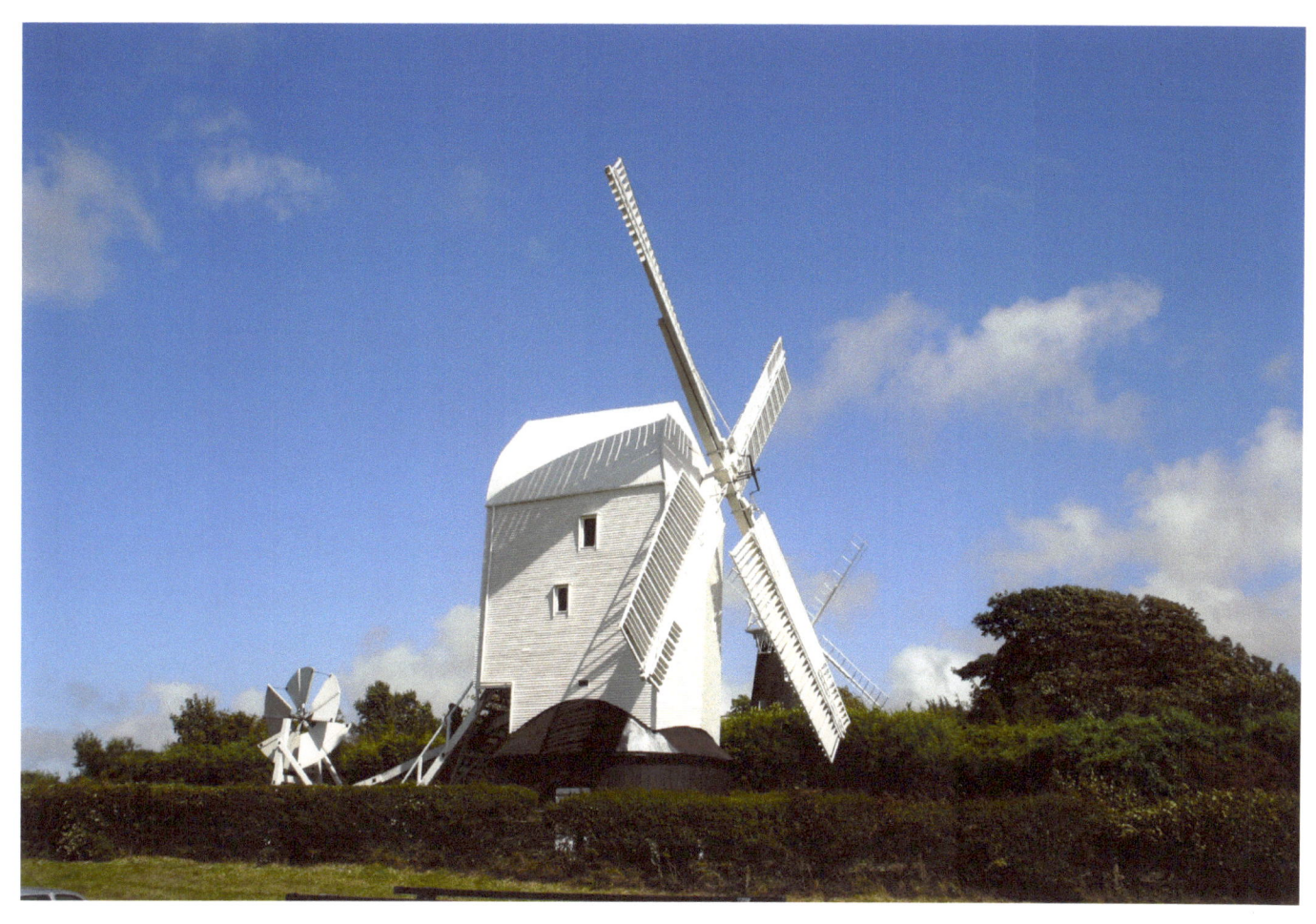

Jill Mill

Forget me not that's what they say
With yellow eyes a-glow
Remember me and I'll make sure
Your vases overflow

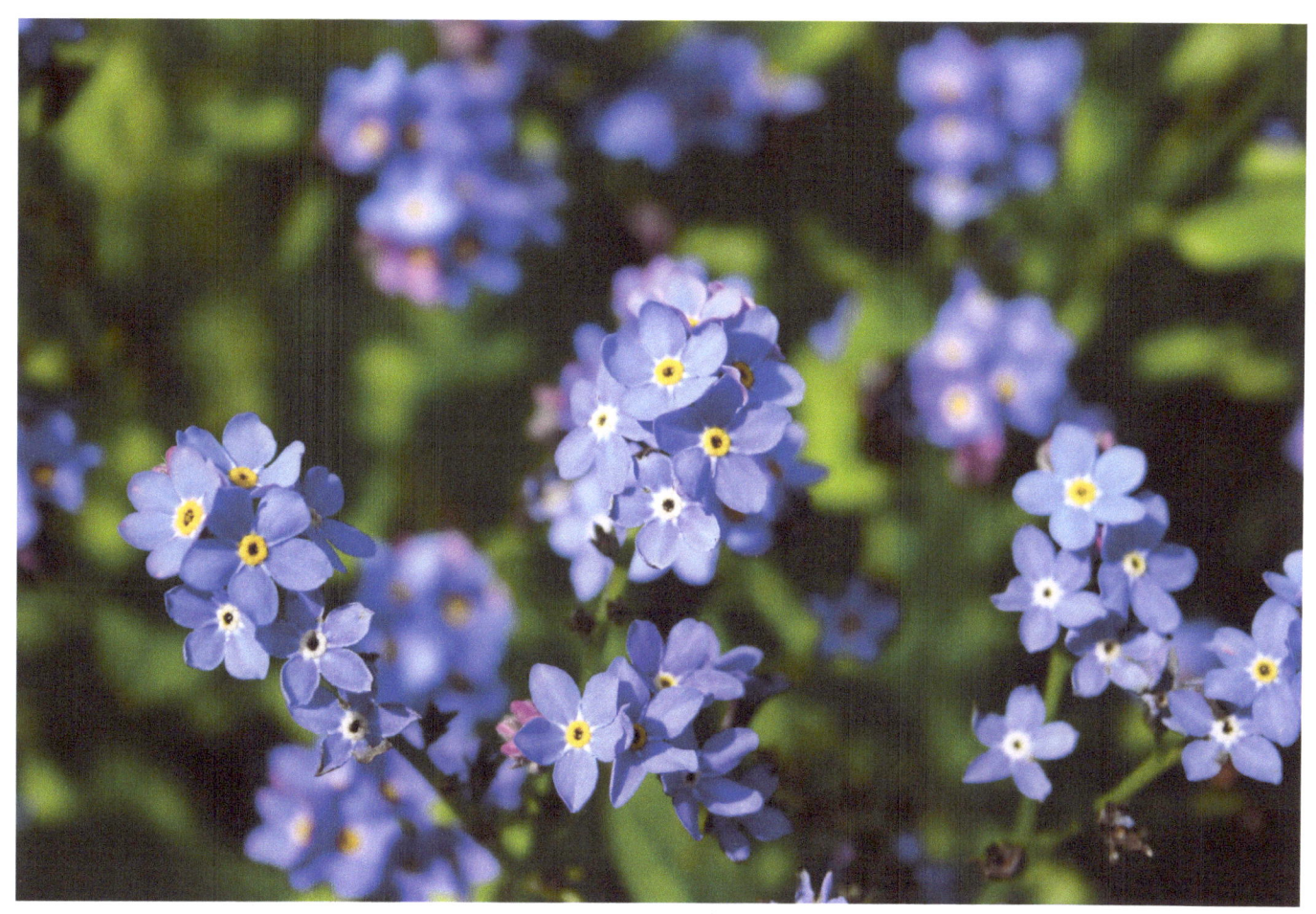

Forget Me Not

Look who's come to say hello
His nose all soft and wet
Is he saying let's be friends
Although we've never met.

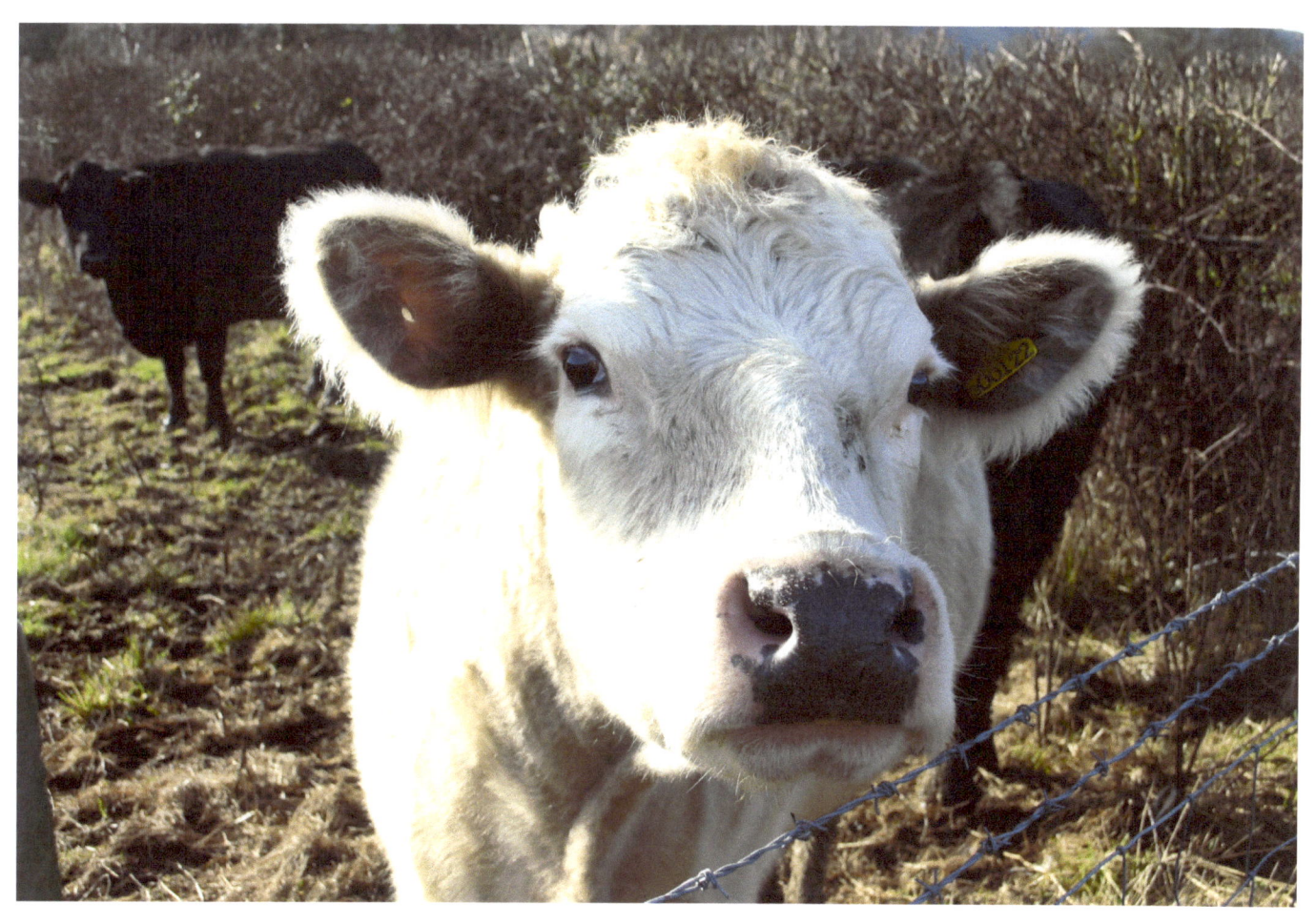

Let's Be Friends

The river winding out of sight
Reflects the glow of morning light
And with its views it hopes to tempt
An oarsman to its boats for rent

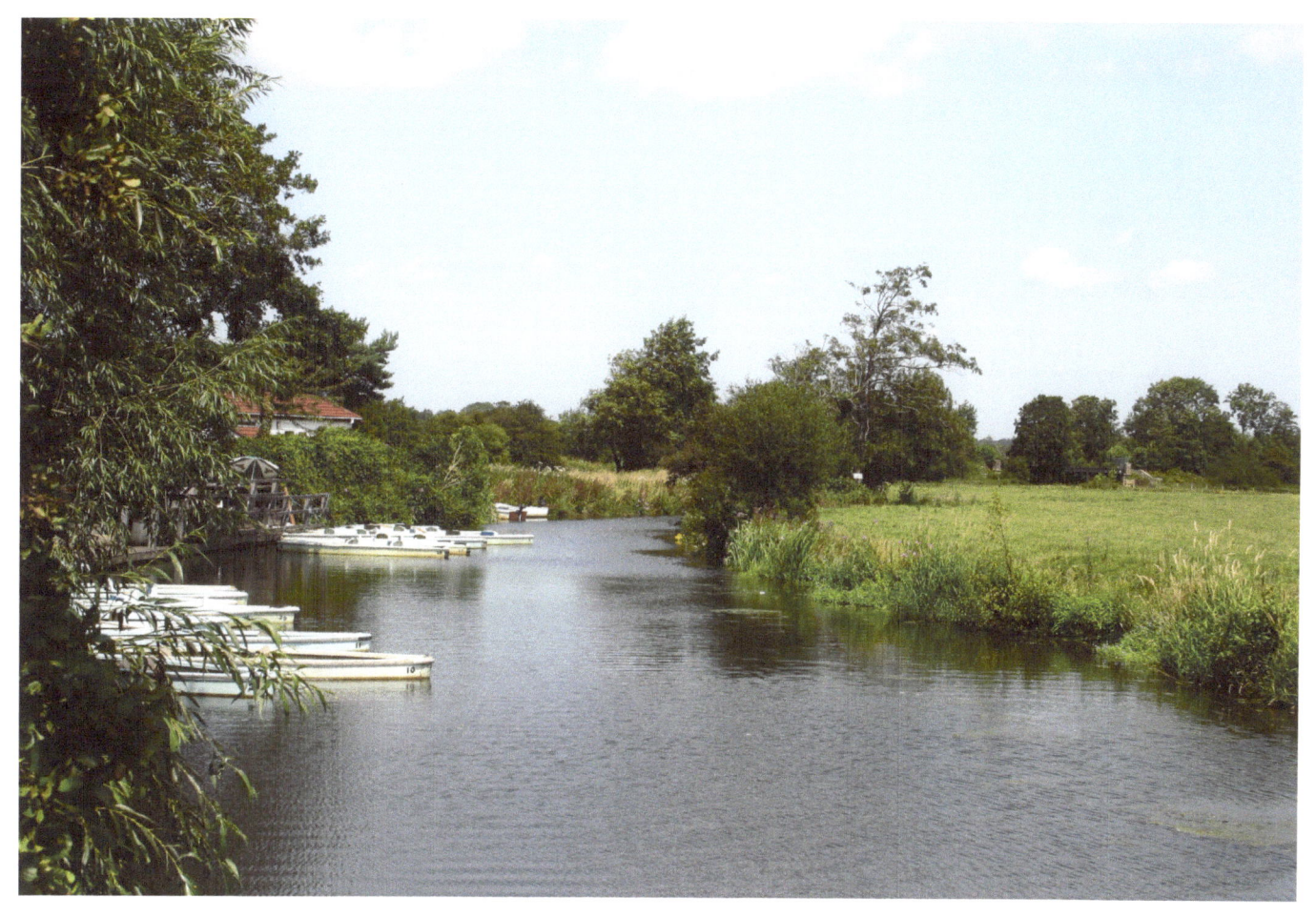

Boats For Rent

Mauve is my colour
Pretty is my game
This is my mauve moment
And it also is my name

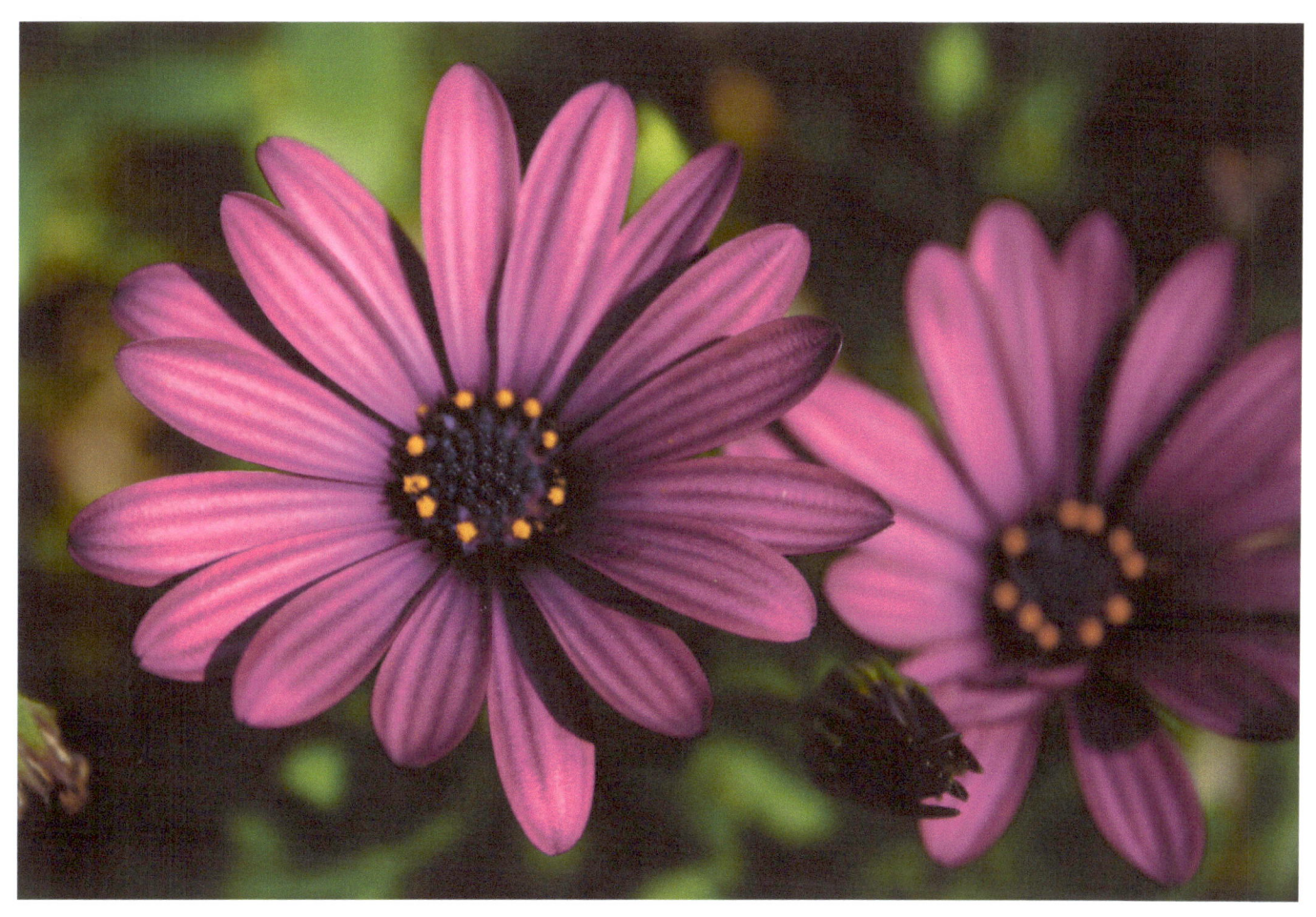

Mauve Moment

Was it sugar icing
that lay before my eyes
The lane under the blanket
Was such a nice surprise

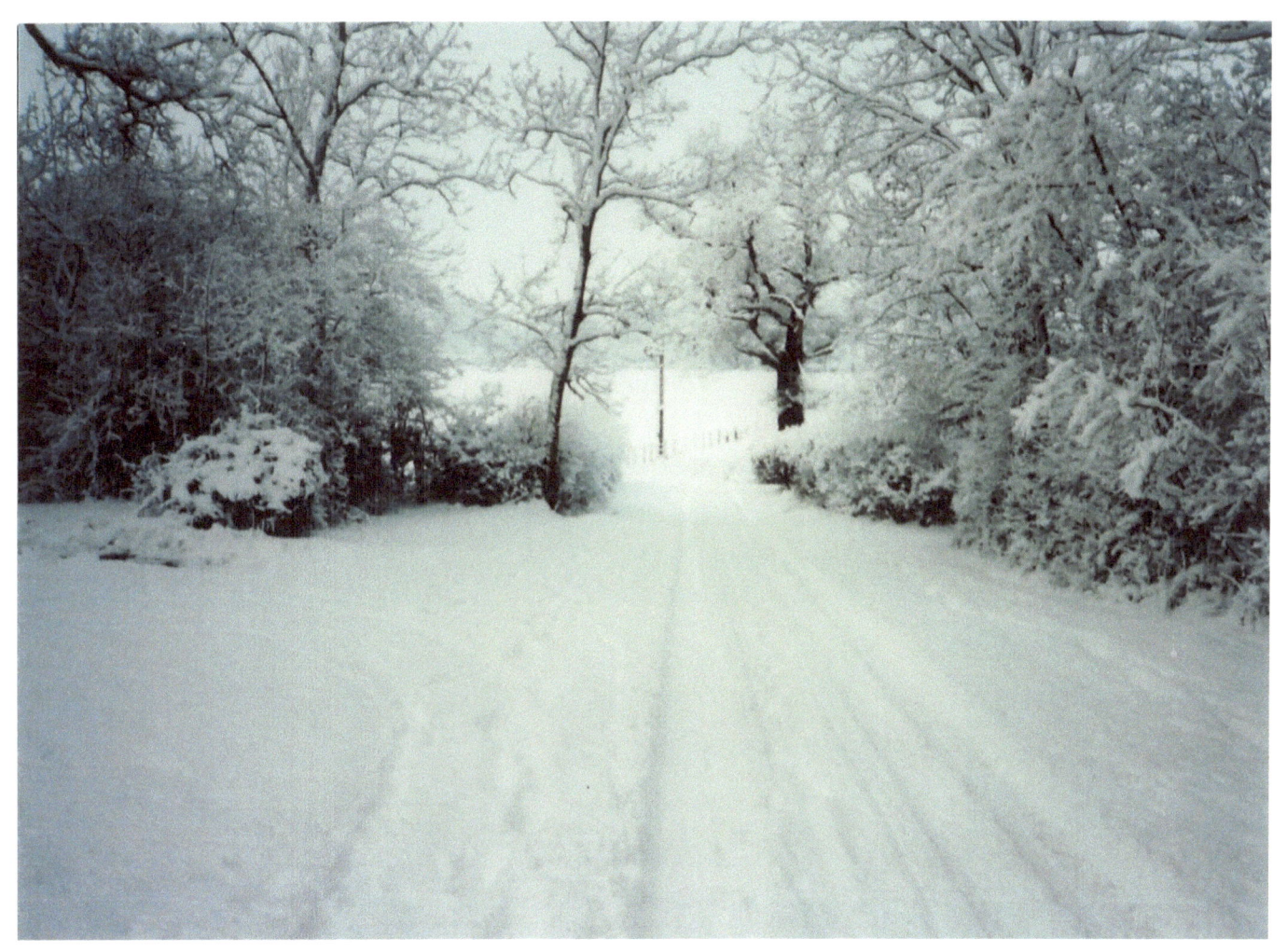

Under The Blanket

See the downs at summer
And drink in all the view
The poppies, hay and greenery
And sky of silver blue

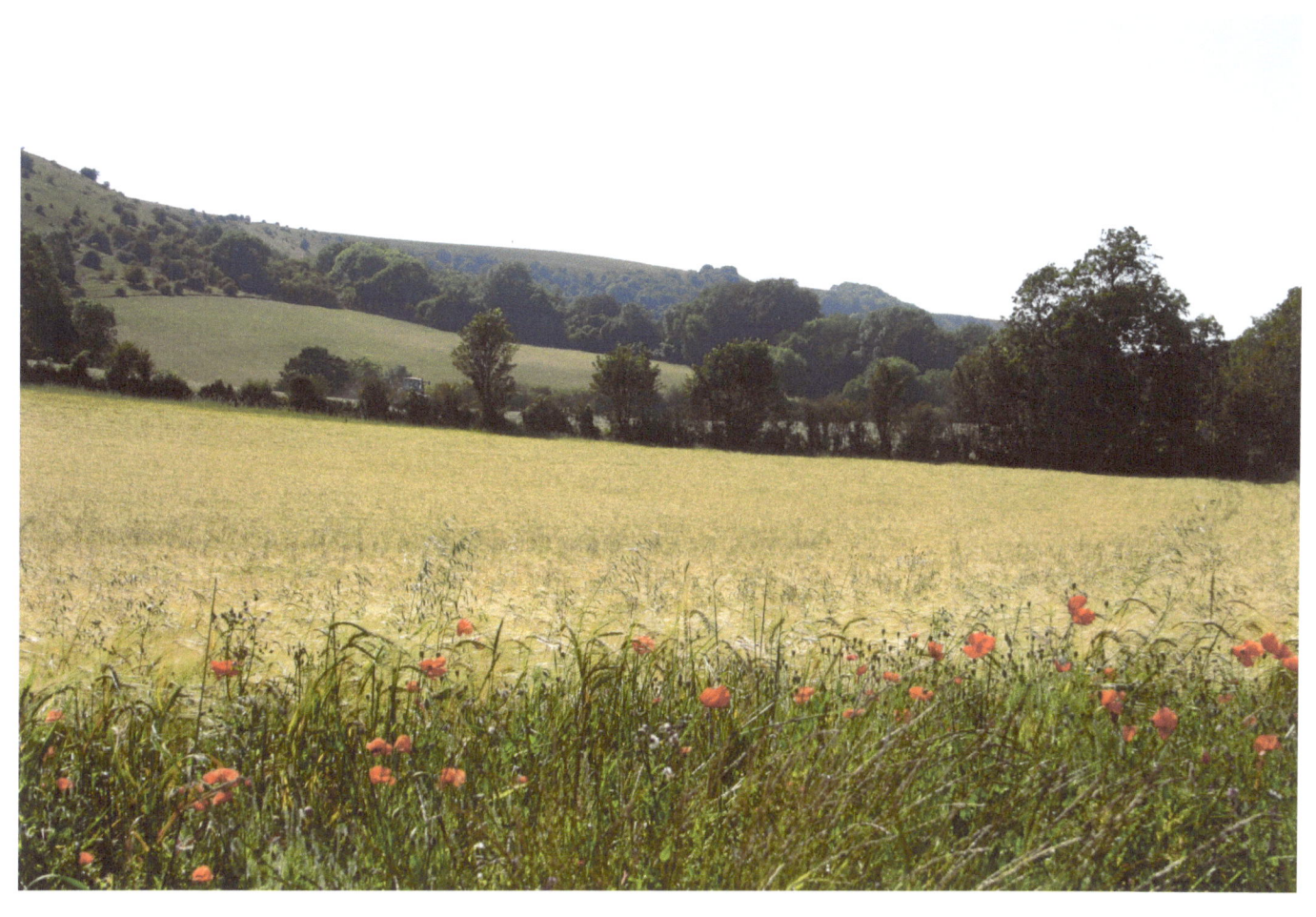

Downs At Summer

Autumn days along the lane
With leaves now turning gold
Shows the local at its best
In colours to behold

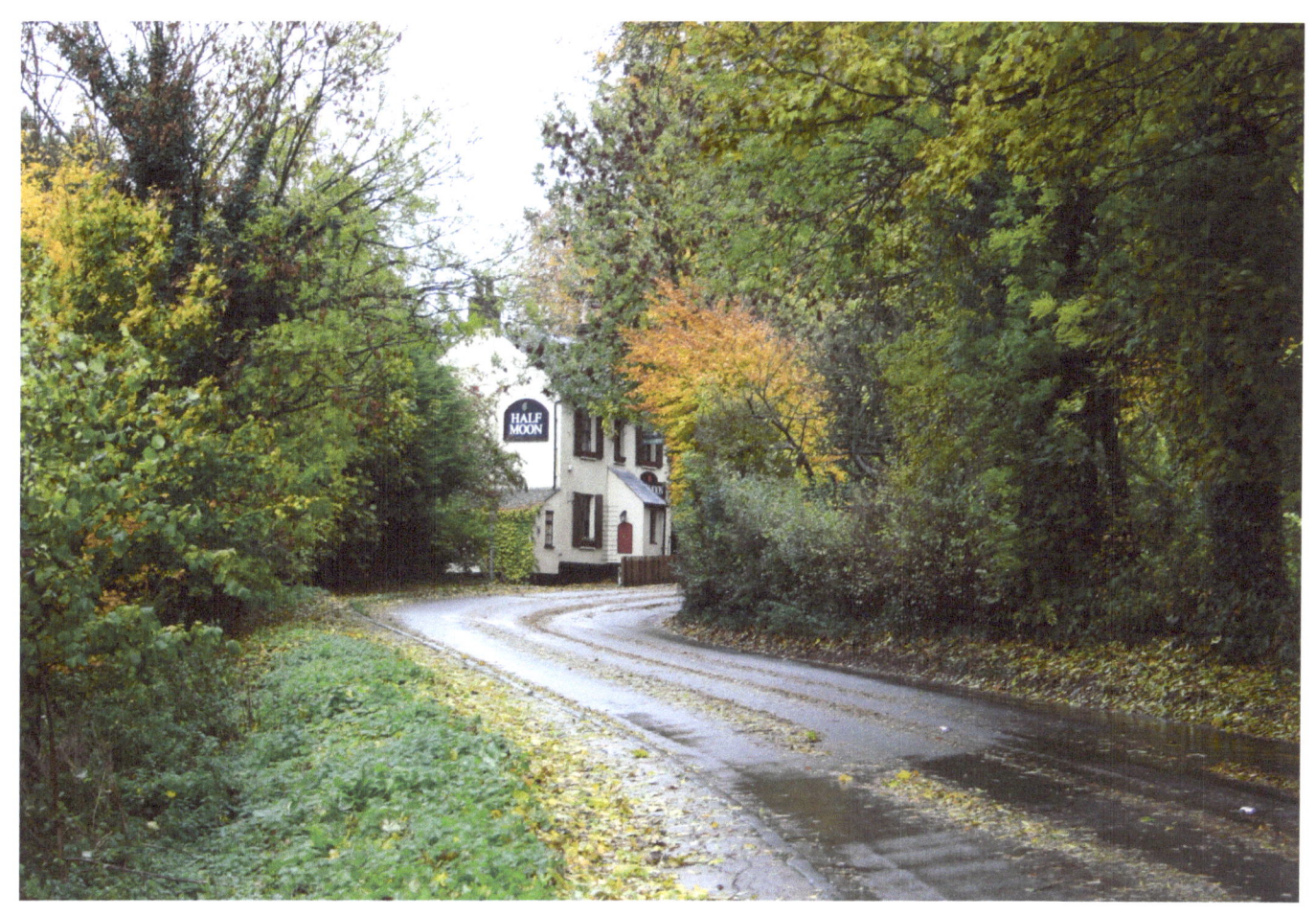

The Local

On petals made of baby pink
The tear drop hangs on tight
And well before an eye can blink
It disappears from sight

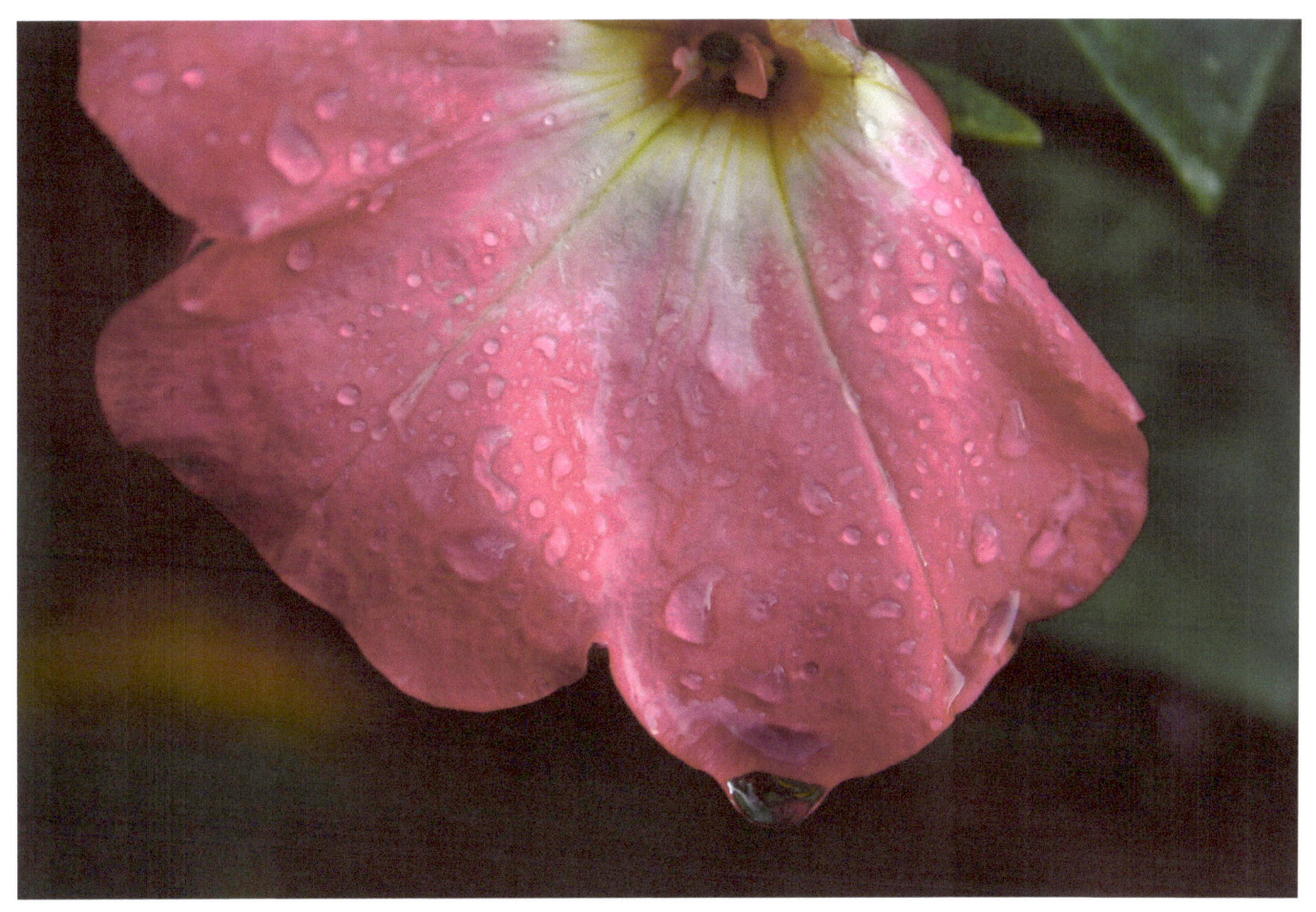

Tear Drop

Winter sunset, winter views
Take away the winter blues
Silhouetting charcoal trees
Waiting for their new year leaves

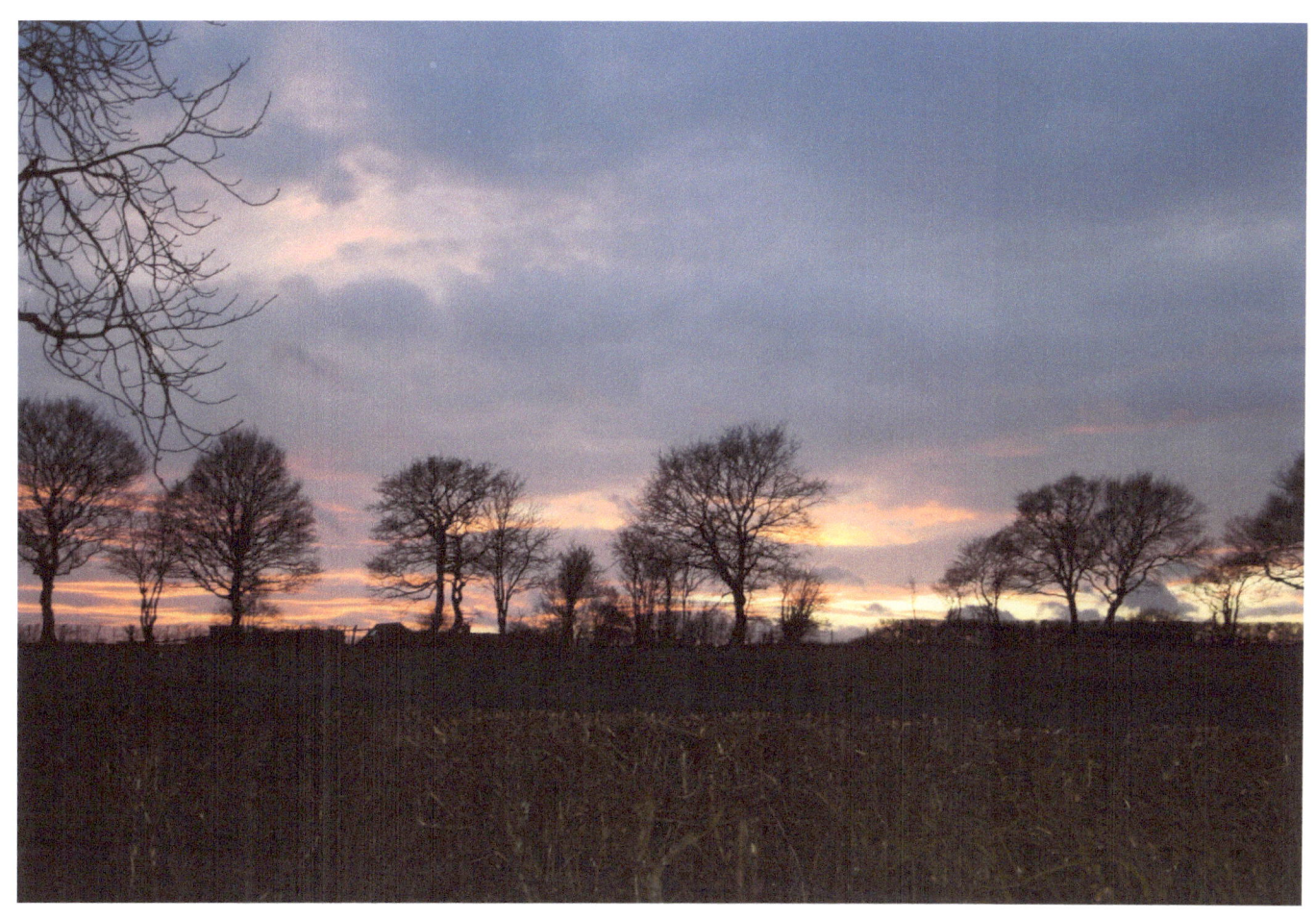

Winter Sunset

Illuminated in its glory
Looking so forlorn
The little church stands firm
To face the calm before the storm

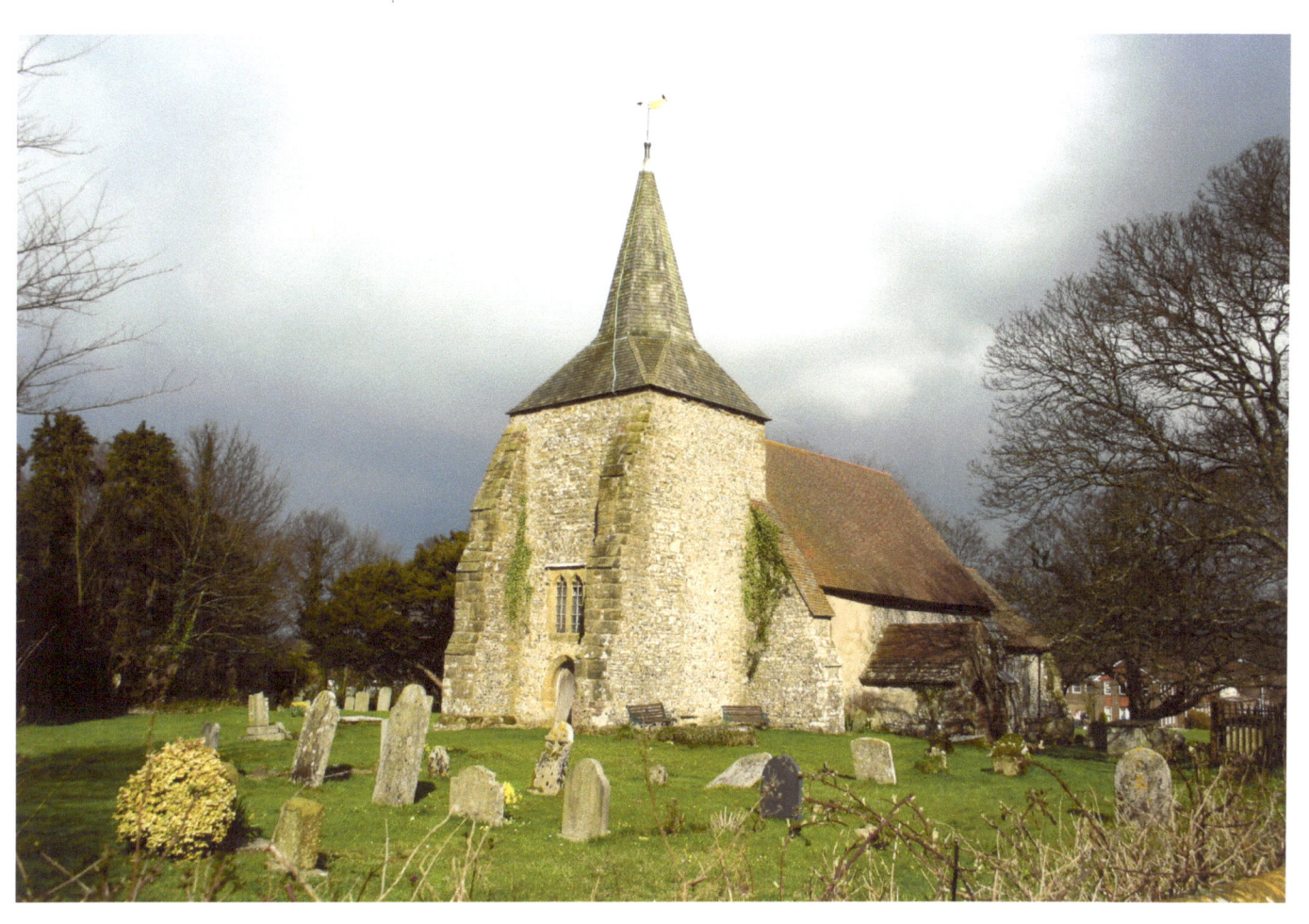

Calm Before The Storm

The woven branches form the arch
That leads you down the lane
The journey takes you to the downs
And brings you back again

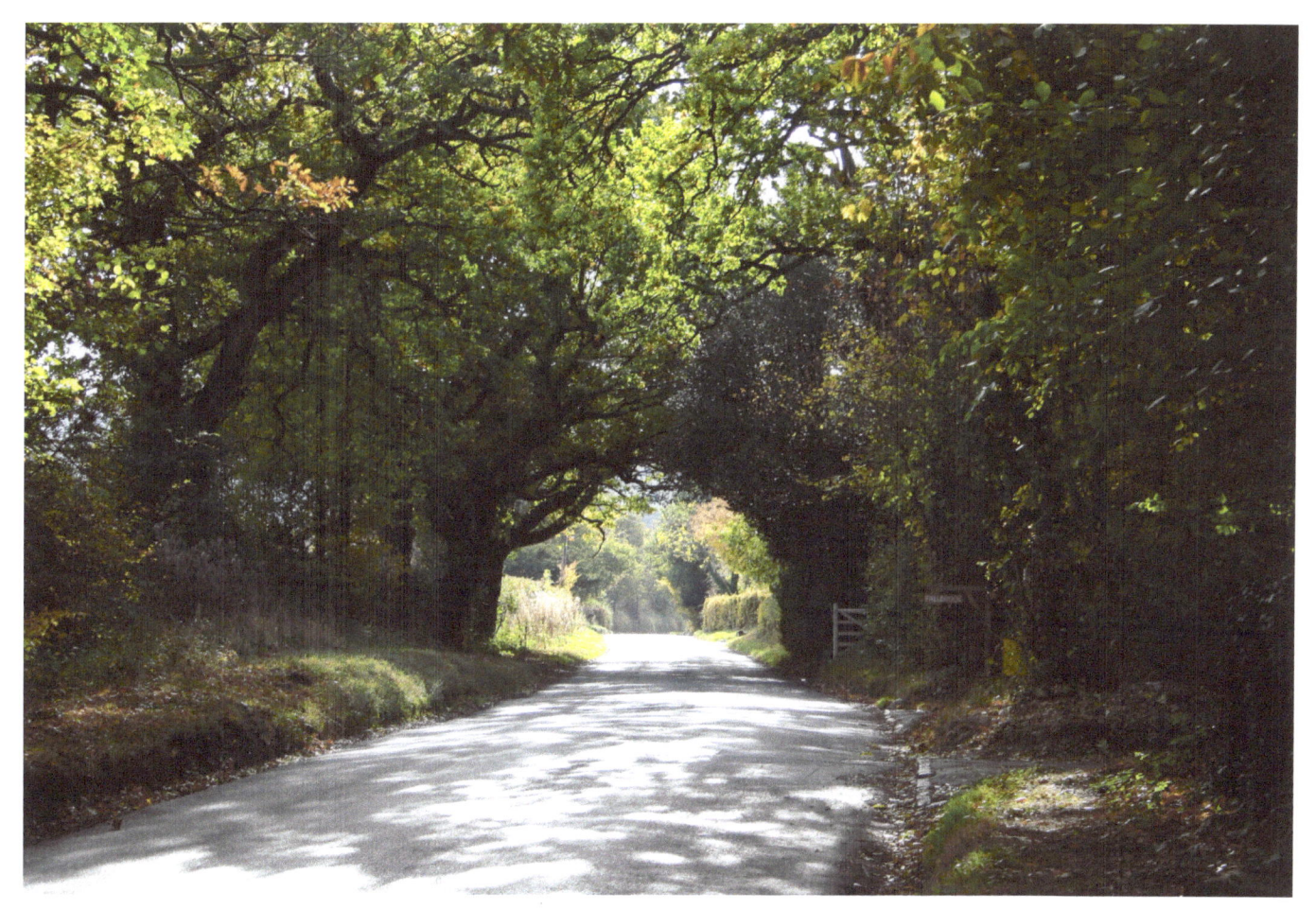

Down The Lane

Evening falls, the sun is setting
Memories of the day to hold
Moving on but not forgetting
Wonders of the rolling gold

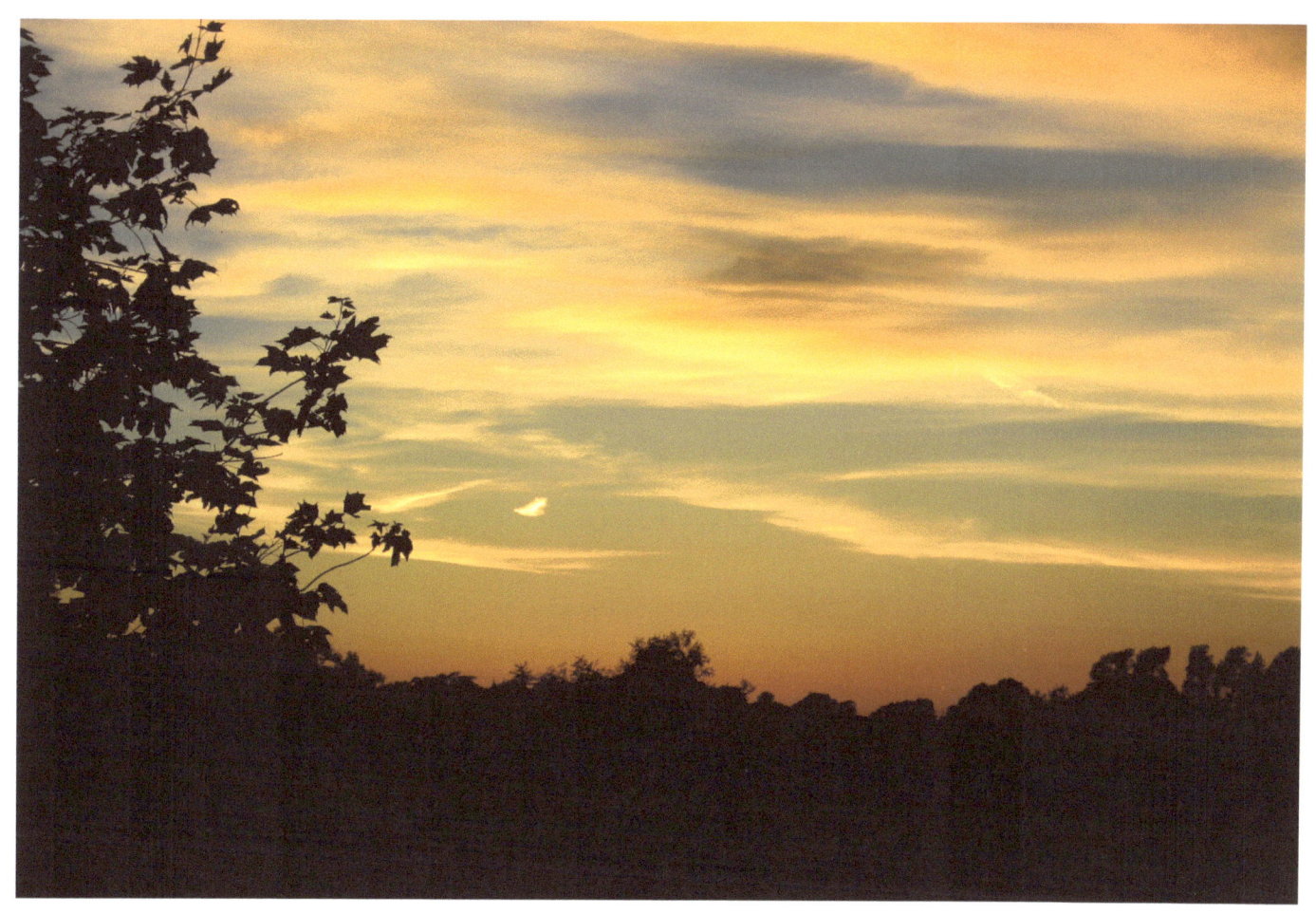

Rolling Gold

With boughs aloft for all to see
The old oak tree stands tall
Who's sat beneath this canopy
In Summer and in Fall

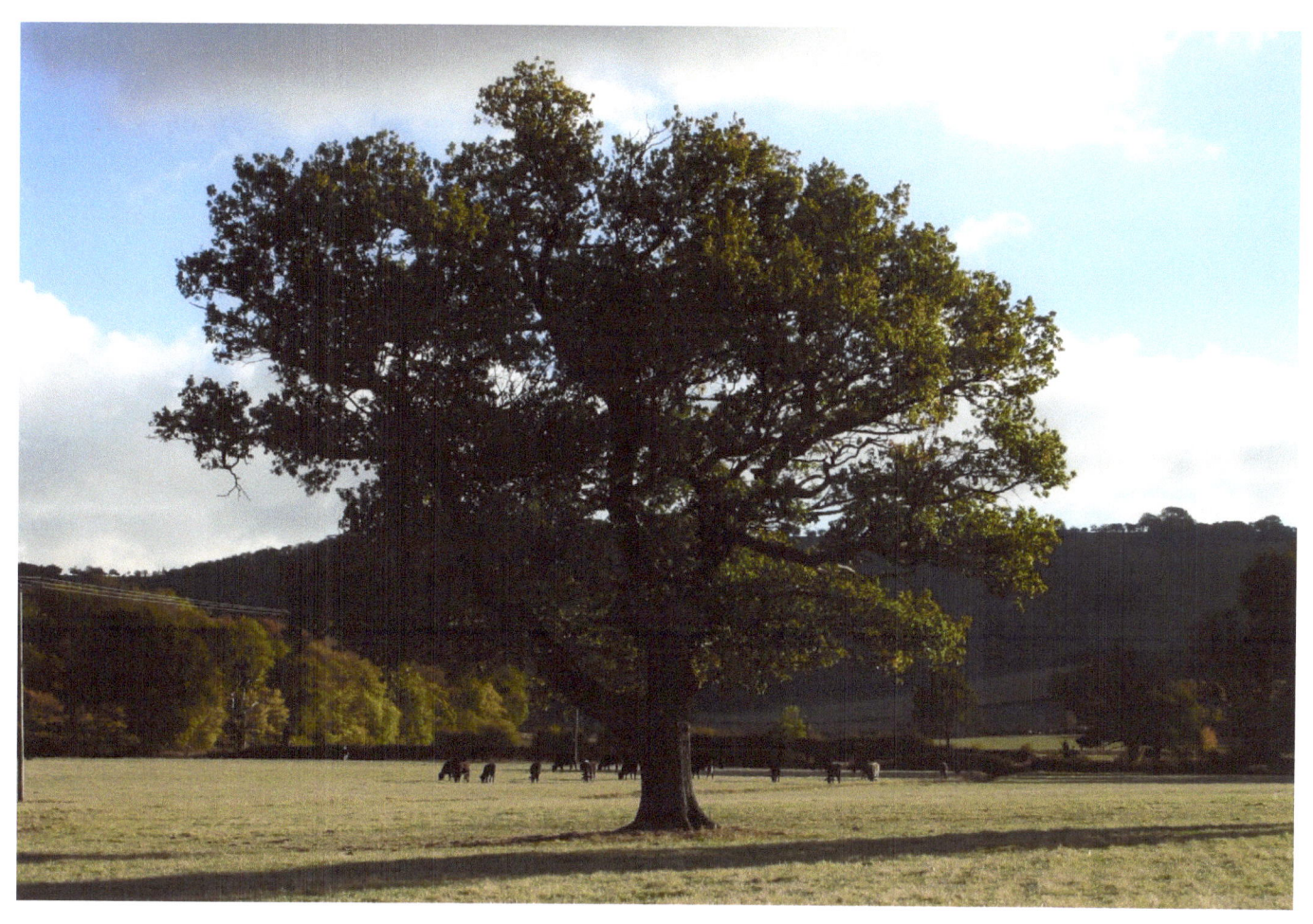

The Old Oak Tree